Jill,

THE HERO'S JOURNEY:

DELIVER YOURSELF
FROM EVIL

May your days be filled w/ light.

Thank you for sharing the Journey,

Chauncey McGlathery

THE HERO'S JOURNEY:
DELIVER YOURSELF FROM EVIL

CHAUNCEY **MCGLATHERY**

KEEN VISION PUBLISHING

Cover Design: by Triv ilovedesignsbytriv@gmail.com

Printed in the United States of America
Keen Vision Publishing, LLC
www.publishwithKVP.com
ISBN: 978-1-948270-93-9

For my dad and all of the heroes brave enough to deliver themselves from evil.

TABLE OF CONTENTS

INTRODUCTION

If we want greater clarity in our purpose or deeper and more meaningful spiritual lives, vulnerability is the path.

Brene Brown

My father was an amazing man. Some remember him as a rocket scientist. Others knew him as the Baptist pastor of the same church for half a century. Many even reflect on him as a patriot. My father was many things to many people, but most never knew that he was a sharecropper.

Did my father hide this part of his identity? *Absolutely not.*

He was not embarrassed about it at all. He had an inordinate pride about his training ground. Even though he eventually left the cotton field for the Redstone Arsenal, he was always proud of his fieldwork.

That part of my father's identity played a big role in how I became who I am. He made major moves, executed his master plan, and became the man he wanted to be before any of his kids were born. Once he and my mom had children, he was already working for NASA. However, even as a senior Aerospace and Systems Engineer, he remained, all his life and in all his endeavors, a man of agriculture — a man of the field. Everything he instructed and demanded his kids to do was, in a very explicit sense, guidelines and warnings so we would never fear going where he had already been — in the cotton field.

Wherever he was, my father was determined to be *the best*. Knowing my father's drive is critical for understanding his identity and how he shaped my siblings and me. He never accepted anything less than everybody's best. That is why, for most of my life, the only thing I ever needed was his approval. If my father gave his nod of approval, that meant it was indeed my best.

And he knew my best.

My father watched me do all kinds of things. The public's approval always came much easier than his, and he often reminded me of that whenever he suspected I was becoming full of myself. Regardless of how well I thought I had done, I never knew the truth until my dad gave his rating. People naturally clap to be polite to whoever is on the stage, so public approval was never my measure of excellence. His feedback told me exactly how well I had performed.

I will never forget the first time my father gave me his nod of approval. Since childhood, I was constantly on a stage, speaking, performing, and/or singing. I did my first solo in elementary school at Madison Academy, in what was then called the Spring Coronation. It was a time for each class to showcase the best of what they had learned in creative arts. I sang "The Impossible Dream" from *Man of La Mancha*.

It was a moment I will never forget. The lights were dimmed. The class was downstage, and I was upstage, front and center, with a spotlight shining down in the narrow space around me. When I finished singing, the crowd roared with praise. At the time, it was the loudest noise I had ever heard a crowd make.

"Dad, what did you think?" I asked my father after the show. *"Yeah. It was okay,"* my father replied. *"You sang better than you did at home."*

People threw flowers. Many of them stood to their feet and cheered. Some even wiped tears from their eyes as they clapped. However, my father's response to my performance was sober. He maintained that attitude throughout my life.

The only other time I recall gaining my father's approval was when I graduated from law school. Even then, it did not come across as gladness or even happiness. When I looked at his face, I saw resentment. Families from all over the world had traveled to Howard University in Washington, D.C., to witness my graduating class's ceremony. You would think my father would have been smiling from ear to ear. I had done extremely well in law school and was offered all kinds of opportunities. I don't believe that my father was not proud of me. I think graduating from law school made me independent of his direction, and he was not ready for that. I believe he feared that his opinion would not matter as much to me since our family and community had begun to see me as an independent thinker and resourceful man in my own right. My father was afraid that I would never need anything from him again.

He did not realize, and neither did I, that even with all of the pomp and circumstance, I still needed his approval. At that time in my life, I did not have the mental capacity to consider that I needed his approval. I did not even know to communicate that I still needed him.

In 2016, my father passed away. Though I was a fully grown adult with experiences under my belt, I still needed him. His death was difficult. I was not upset with him for not fighting harder to stay alive. I was devastated that I no longer had the choice to rely on him.

For three years after his death, I woke up every day feeling like Isaac. I was on the altar, but Abraham was nowhere to be found. Who am I, if not Isaac? I never really thought about my identity past my relationship with my father. I never considered what might happen when we finally came down the mountain.

MY IDENTITY

Who was I without my father? After my father's death, I filled my schedule completely. The goal was to ensure that I would not have a moment to think, much less breathe. For three or four months, I distracted myself. I spent my days in a rat race, doing stuff at church and managing various projects all over the city. If I had not fallen desperately ill, I would have continued down this destructive path.

My sickness forced me to come to terms with the life I had lived through the eyes of my father. As I laid in the hospital bed, I realized how distraught I was. I knew exactly what my father would do had he been there. As I waited for a diagnosis, I imagined my father's hand resting on my chest as they had so many times before when I was a kid recovering from bouts with strep throat.

He had used those hands so many times to clap for me in the crowded stands of the Huntsville Recreational Football League. His hands also communicated terror when he had to discipline me. At my weakest point, I knew exactly where his hands would have been...one laying heavily upon my chest, and the other at his side.

Now, my father hadn't consoled me like that since I was a kid. But it was such a critical part of who I knew him to be. He was not just a stern dad; he was also very loving. The power with which he loved his children was like nothing I have ever seen before. It was a biblical love. He was the best father. I can't imagine having had a better protector, father, provider, or teacher.

So, when did I become *Chauncey*? When did I find my identity apart from my father?

I was secretly becoming me the entire time. When I left Alabama after college and moved to D.C. for law school, I relegated space in my life margins to develop my sense of self and become Chauncey. Moving to D.C. was huge for my personal growth and development. I had to live and create an identity in spaces, towns, cities, and states where no one had a clue who my father was. I had to learn how to do everything outside of his sphere of influence.

Though his legacy no longer went before me into rooms, I took his presence. No one had a presence quite like my father, and I'm glad I was able to learn that from him. That presence opened doors for me in D.C., then in New York, and later in Boston. It did not matter where I was, whether I was in the courtroom, the sanctuary, the classroom, or on the stage — I strived to be the best. Even when doing something for the first time, I was lavished with praise from every instructor, teacher, or director. I was just like my father when he was in the field, even though my labor was on a stage. I was *the best* and refused to settle for anything less than that.

MY BOTTOM

At every performance and every task, I endeavored and pressed for perfection. That's all I knew to do. Though he could not see me, I could feel my father at every step on every stage. I could feel his nod of approval, and it made me feel whole. So in being perfect, I was myself. I knew I was present and valuable because I was exactly what I had been trained to be: perfect.

In my scenario, I was present and whole when I was perfect. There was only one issue with this perspective. What would happen when I could not be perfect? You guessed it. I could not handle it.

After my father died and I became ill, I had to confront this problem face to face. It was not the first time I'd dealt with disappointment, but it was the first time I was rendered helpless and unable to change my circumstances. I could not take "the course" again. I could not re-enroll, re-apply, move, or start over. I was stuck like the coyote under the Road Runner's anvil. I was stuck, not under the weight of a loving hand, but of a deafening disappointment that I did not know how to lift.

Getting sick was the first time that perfection was completely outside my reach. Every other time, when I disappointed myself and failed to reach perfection, I could still see it, no matter how far the distance. I would figure out the process, learn the formula, and go after perfection again. However, when I was sick, there were no steps. I was on an island, surrounded by an ocean. I did not have a clue who I was. I was confused, like a ship without a sail, like an astronaut without a shuttle. I was unanchored, and I was floating, being pushed and pulled by every wind, current, ocean, and idea. And what's worse, I had no clue what would happen next.

I felt into and through consciousness. I seemed to travel far away from how I had learned to live. I fell for so long that eventually, I just stopped falling. Eventually, I was at the bottom.

Someone once asked me, *"When you hit your bottom, what was it like? Was there finally peace for you?"* I wish. It was not peaceful exactly, but it was quiet. There was no one there to tell me how I should live.

The doctors had tested me for every cancer, virus, bacteria, organ failure, heart condition, and brain trauma they could think of. Yet, they found nothing that explained my illness. Much of what happened to me in that hospital room I'll never remember. But I remember the day my brother visited me for what the doctors assumed would be the last time. It was the day after I had a series of almost fatal seizures.

I don't remember most of what happened that day, but I discussed it with my mother and her sisters. The doctors, who still had no idea what was wrong with me, told my family that I had suffered a series of seizures and had to be placed in the ICU. The doctors explained that the next seizure would put me in a coma, one from which I would never awake. My mother was advised to call the family so everyone could say their final goodbyes.

Everyone visited, but I did not realize the significant of their presence. However, when my brother came into the room, I opened my eyes. I'll never forget what I saw and felt from my brother's presence. He was standing over me, looking like a descendant of slaves, walking into the Legacy Museum in Montgomery. His countenance could be described as that of a Holocaust survivor walking around Auschwitz. You would have thought I had been in a coma for six months. He looked as if he had been exhausted, having conquered hell and high water just long enough to bid me goodbye. I had never seen that look on my brother's face before. He inherited his disposition from our father. They are both built like emotional fortresses—impenetrable. Until that moment, I did not even know he was capable of showing that much emotion. But that day, when I looked into my brother's eyes, I knew I was at the bottom of my identity.

MY CONFIDENCE

I had a choice to make. I could die, or I could get up. I had lost the secret recipe for my life. I did not have the formula for perfection anymore. Since I was already at the bottom, stopping was a feasible option. After all, I had accomplished 99% of all I had planned to do. I'd had a good run — a couple of degrees and a marriage. What more could I have asked for?

Lying there, down to nothing, I still had the nerve to be confident. I believed that though I had hit rock bottom, my life was not done. The life I was created to live had not reached its end. I had no clue where that confidence came from, but I was convicted to believe there was more for me.

When my family informed the doctors that I was awake, they rushed into the room to speak with my family and me. I don't remember much about that day, but my Aunt Florence, who has always been the best truth-teller in our family, remembers that day vividly. With great excitement, she shared every detail upon my request.

"Look, this is it." my aunt recalled the doctor saying to me. *"You need to get your affairs in order. Your family is here to say goodbye. You're not leaving this hospital alive. I have to tell you the truth because it's my responsibility. This is goodbye."*

After his comment, my aunt said that she looked at me, and determination slowly swept across my being. She realized I was not close to an end. By that point, I had been in a hospital bed for a couple of weeks. I had been extremely frustrated during my entire stay. Every time the doctors came into the room, they spoke about me but rarely spoke to me. However, after the doctor's statement, my aunt recalls me becoming very calm. Though they never gave me the floor to speak, on that day, I took it.

"Ohhhh, nah." My aunt said I drawled out slowly. I imagine that I went to an old place in my mind. It was a place that I'm sure my ancestors visited a million times before. It's a refuge in the midst of infinite ocean storms. That old place is like the sanctuary in the soul, comforting and assuring you when all the evidence is against you. At the very bottom, I found that place, and in it, my confidence.

"What did you say?" The doctor asked.

"Oh, nah." My aunt said I replied. *"What? No! It's not gonna happen like that. This is not as big of a thing for me as you think it is. I'm not exactly sure what all is going to happen between now and me leaving this hospital, but I'm definitely going to be leaving this hospital. In a few days. Because I've got to get to the life I have not lived yet."*

All of this was just a prelude. I actually said those words. I had that confidence. For the first time, I had a true sense of what it meant to be present, here, on this planet, and in this universe.

Hitting rock bottom allowed me to realize what mattered and what did not. It was not about the awards or accolades. The positions and experiences I'd had no longer mattered. Now, my days are relaxed. I'm not anxious about what I have or who is around. If I have appointments or meetings, whether everything happens or nothing happens, my attitude and reflection about the day remain the same.

MY BEING

I no longer judge my days based on my accomplishments or what I achieved. Now, I base the value of my days on my awareness. Instead of asking myself, *"Chauncey, what did you achieve today?"* I now consider, *"What did I hear today for the first time? What did I learn?"* I hope that after reading this book, you will see the treasure in rating your days with a similar rubric.

Before I hit bottom, I was very much an island. I was an unrepentant solo act, a one-man show. I did not need anybody or anything to make me happy, and I loved this about myself. I was good all by myself.

That would have always been true about me until I realized being alone was not healthy. I can't move, live, or breathe without everybody, and everything created, contributing to my existence daily. Before hitting bottom, I was not ever really independent. I just enjoyed the illusion that I was. It gave me a sense of control of my fate and my destiny. Honestly, I always thought to myself, *"If they aren't my father, they do not matter to my success."*

Now, I have more joy. Even deeper than joy, I have more

me. I am more myself than I ever thought I could be. I talk, introduce myself, and engage others with more sincerity. I am truly interested in discovering not our differences or distinctions but our similarities.

Every day, I find gems in every experience. I have a cool part-time food delivery job where I get to walk in and out of restaurants, residences, and workplaces, picking up orders and making deliveries. I am in and out of different living, working, and social settings that, in my previous life, would have meant nothing to me. The old Chauncey would have hated it. He would have never even applied for the job.

In my past life, I was the gem. Now, I am the gem hunter. From a value and life perspective, giving myself away, I end up with more than I had before.

Anyone who would dare to apply the five principles of deliverance I discuss in this book will get more out of life than they ever anticipated. If you are anything like I was, you are an island, a one-man show, a *good all by yourself* type of person. However, this practice will help you realize that you can not move the way you want to move in isolation. You are not wired for it. Someone who follows this practice will soon realize that we were not meant to live separately from everyone else.

We are all connected, inherently and eternally.

Now I will not just say that you will have more joy, although truer words could not be spoken. You will have something even deeper than joy. You will have more you. Do you know what I mean? There will be more of you in everything. You will be more present. You will introduce yourself and engage with others with true interest to discover similarities. Every day and in every experience, you will search for gems. You will be pleased to find them everywhere you dare to look.

CHAPTER ONE:
PERFORMING

There is no better teacher than adversity. Every defeat, every heartbreak, every loss, contains its own seed, its own lesson on how to improve your performance next time.

Malcolm X

As I decided to write this book, I was reminded of the standard of behavior impressed upon me by my father. My father was known to always be his best. Whether he was in the cotton field or working as an engineer for NASA at Redstone Arsenal, he was the best. It defined him at home, church, work, and in the community.

He gave me a standard of living that required that I always be *my best*.

Even as a kid on stage being celebrated by my hometown, I waited until I got my father's nod of approval to know if I had truly done my best. Because I learned this fundamental lesson early and found great success in building an identity around excellence, I literally took the show on the road. I approached every relationship and opportunity, for half of my adult life, with this same standard of excellence. I also required everyone I encountered to live up to this standard and only valued those who appeared to be giving 100% in every endeavor. This practice was detrimental to my personal growth and caused me to be emotionally isolated from my friends and co-workers. I was an island in the middle of an ocean, isolated, disconnected, and alone.

Now that I have begun the work that we will discuss in this book, I no longer view myself as a gem because of my ability to push others to be *the best*. I focus on the fact that there are gems everywhere, waiting to be discovered. Being *the best* requires a level of performance that we aren't always able to sustain. In this first chapter, we will tackle the fascinating topic of performance. As I pull back the covers and reveal how I adopted an unfruitful performance mindset, I hope you will gain the insight to deal with your own.

For quite some time, there was a place within me that required an external display of value to know my worth. But where was it? What was it inside me that felt so inadequate? What made me feel so unsafe that I needed to be doing something great to feel valued, accepted, and loved?

Here is the perfect example. Actors are typically people who put on a role or character of another person to tell someone's story. Whenever I witness a good performance, I forget the effort. The distance between the actor and the character collapses to zero. When I see a good performance, I feel like I'm witnessing the truth personified. I feel like I'm witnessing a galaxy under construction. I feel as though God is allowing mere mortals to commune in the heavens. It is as if the performer can tap into a portal where all the spirits of masterpieces dwell, a heavenly gallery curated by the Genius

Designer himself.

A good performer may not ever be sad when performing a sad scene. But if the audience believes the performer is sad, as evidenced by a falling tear, an appropriately shaky voice, or apparent lump in the throat, they are all as satisfied as if they were in heaven. Alternatively, if the performer makes the audience experience sadness within themselves, that is *extraordinary.*

An actor who has practiced at being a good performer is power. Their work is very convincing and always believable for the audience, but it is also very dangerous for the actor. Many of the stories that are performed feature characters with real demons. It is hard enough to manage our own evil. Can you imagine taking on somebody else's, even if it were just for a moment?

Before my transformation that brought about this book and before I realized I needed deliverance from my evil, I always considered myself one of the best performers on any stage I touched. It was my legacy. It was my inheritance. I come from a family of great performers.

My dad introduced to me a standard of performance that always required my best, and until he gave his nod of approval, I worked hard for it but never quite held it for long in my grasp. But greatness in my performance was the reason I woke up in the morning.

What started as a virtue became a vice. What started as my good became my evil.

What I performed was not evil. I don't believe that many

things are evil in and of themselves. What made my original performances evil was the motivation I had behind them. My performances were all about me. They were all self-centered. I got on stage to get something I did not already have offstage.I needed validation. I needed praise. I needed attention, then celebration. And once I got it, I could not get enough of it.

Onstage, I got something from the audience that I needed in real-life — a sense of adequacy and security. Onstage, I knew I was good enough. I knew I was talented enough. I knew that my shortcomings were invisible under the lights. I was protected, celebrated, and loved. I freely expressed those feelings while I was onstage during the performance and well after wardrobe and makeup were gone.

While at dinner at a restaurant in Boston, an audience member left her family's table to greet me. *"You were fantastic,"* she said to me. I hated to be interrupted, but I needed her to say every praiseworthy thing she could remember about my performance.

One year, I auditioned for over thirty shows and was cast in over ten. I would have three rehearsals for three different shows in three different cities. I would leave a performance then head straight to a rehearsal. I could not be away from the stage. I could not get enough. Even when I went home, I could not sleep. In my head, I relived the desperate joy of the applause, and the words of praise new fans or old friends would shower on me.

Today, everyone says that whatever you do on stage should not be a performance, particularly in sacred spaces or with friends or family. *"You should not perform,"* they say.

"You should just be." Be? Really? You want me to get on a microphone in front of hundreds of people and *just be?* I don't think you do, but it sounds good.

Before I realized that I needed deliverance, I spent a lot of time trying to find that space where I was not performing on the microphone but just being. I now realize that everything you do in life is a performance — not only artistic, high-talent, high-skilled things but also mundane and ordinary things. Even love is a performance.

John 3:16 tells us that because God loves us, he gave. In the Judeo-Christian narrative, Jesus was not at the scene of his crucifixion being his best Zenself. He was on a cross, dying. If it actually happened, it was the greatest performance ever recorded in history. Now, I understand. I don't want to be delivered from a performance mentality. I want to be delivered from bad performances.

I define a bad performance in three ways. First, you can fail to deliver the work required by the role. This is the most obvious form of a bad performance and not the particular problem I had. It's not only what you do on stage that makes a bad performance. You can deliver a "perfect performance" that receives acclaim, awards, and endless adoration. Therefore, the second form of a bad performance is not about the what, but about your why. If your motivation flows from your needs instead of the needs of those around you, that "perfect performance" is fatally flawed.

Thirdly, an otherwise perfect performance can be fatally flawed if you can't emotionally leave the stage at the end of the performance. You refuse to leave because you can't rest in your own greatness. You require the cover of the character or role you play.

Something that character possesses is missing inside of you. Just as the actors onstage have to deal with that character's issues, when you bring that character home, everyone around you has to learn how to deal with that character as well. And worse yet, the version of you that they love is no longer available because you have traded down to become a lesser version of yourself.

Although there are actors who stay in character throughout a movie production, they take a huge risk in doing so. Actors' families often tell stories of how they hated their loved one the entire time they shot a movie because they became that character. So if the character was mean, so they had to be mean. Since the actor never left the stage, they brought the character home with them for their families to deal with.

How did I begin the process of overcoming my evil in performance? I had to learn how to perform out of the work I'd done on myself. Great performances are not manufactured externally. They flow forth as a natural expression of the actor inside the character. So, you may ask, how did I learn to nurture myself the same way I nurtured a character? I had to prepare for my life performances just as I prepared to play a character in a play. I examined my motivations and got my insecurities, lies, previous roles, and false characters out of the way.

I literally changed my character. I put myself in the main character's role and gave myself everything I needed to be whole and complete. As an actor, I took copious notes, and I allowed the director of the production to teach me about the character's motivation.

Offstage, I am learning to deliver myself from my evil. I repeat the same process I used as an actor, except this time, for a different Director — my Creator Designer. What He says about me is my new script. I comb the pages of all relevant sacred texts as translated and interpreted. I memorize and rehearse my new lines, and almost immediately, my true self shines forth.

Now, I am training myself the way I would a character. I rehearse in my hearing the things God says about me. Speaking affirmations is my personal performance. I aspire to be great outside of the spotlight, where it counts the most. I don't always wake up feeling strong, loved, and accepted, but I recite that script because I trust my Director.

The Director always has a vision of my scenes that I do not understand. I have worked on shows with over 40 people in the cast. Until the stage is set and the wardrobe and orchestra get in place, you don't know the show. You may have all of your lines, blocking, and songs memorized, but until it all comes together, you still have no idea what the show will look like.

If you try to wait until all of the pieces come together, you will have delayed your preparation. Once it's time to play your part, you will not be prepared. No, you have to trust your Director. Learn your choreography and trust that the Director knows something about your scenes that you don't.

Directors also know the other limitations of every aspect of the production, which have not been revealed to you. You may have an idea, but it's probably better for you to keep quiet and trust your direction. In the end, you are not responsible for how your story plays out. You are only responsible for delivering what was asked of you.

Now that I am on the other side of my deliverance process, my life is different. Even though my performances do not always align with my feelings, they perfectly align with my principles. The more I rehearse offstage by reciting my new script of affirmations, the closer I get to the character the Director had in mind when He cast me. This new and improved character is a worthy addition to the cast and story, but most importantly, he is a better version of me.

When you follow this principle in your life, it will change you too. Even when you don't feel like hearing about someone's day, you will now be eager to extend an ear. You will sit and listen to friends and family, and they will love you for it. You will ask how others are doing, not because YOU need it, but because they do. The love you previously struggled to show will flow naturally and become your most important performance. You will be invested in all that happens around you all day, whether it is about you or not.

Needless to say, this transformation does not happen overnight. I have been working on this new way of performing for about two years, and I am still a work in progress. However, when you commit to doing the work offstage, you will exemplify the work onstage. Slowly, we are all able to become the masterpieces our Director had in mind when He cast us in this great play we call life.

Finally, be careful about the roles you take as a performer. There is an essence inside you that flows without effort, but she hasn't been allowed the freedom to show the world just how spectacular she is. Rehearse the script that is natural to her and nurture her early in the morning, first and foremost. And once her heart is open, you will exceed your every expectation.

AFFIRMATIONS

I am present at this place.

I am connected to the heart of the universe.

I am comfortable sitting and contemplating my purpose.

I am grateful to receive all that is coming my way.

I am eager to strip away all that doesn't belong on my path and seize all that does.

I am ready to share my light with this moment.

CHAPTER TWO:
WINNING

*To be heroic is to be courageous enough to die for something;
to be inspirational is to be crazy enough to live a little.*

Criss Jami, Venus in Arms

In Chapter One, we discussed the benefit of living life from a place of naturally being as opposed to frantically doing. We dispelled the myth that performance is bad altogether, as all of life is a performance. We considered that we don't need deliverance from performance, just bad performance.

Good performances are necessary.

Before my transformation, I lived life under the fallacy that I could perform my way into love. That somehow, if I could show myself to be good enough, I could earn acceptance the same way you earn a trophy for a job well done. This way of thinking caused me to undervalue myself and so many others.

It felt like I carried a cross burdened with the weight of the world, with glimpses of happiness surrounded by glares of despair. I am grateful to be on the other side of that vicious cycle. Once we agree to enter this space, we can move from a life of measured performance into an open life of acceptance.

Once you live from a place of acceptance, every day is *a joy*.

From the lessons of history, I've learned that there are a thousand ways to win and a million different types of wins. What makes a good win? Historically, I have always thought of a winner as someone who has worked harder and achieved more than everybody else. Now, I think of winning as something much more personal than the final public result. I think of the process. A good win is not about the results, but the cost to get them.

Good wins result from the deliberate and intentional application of values that results in better health for all affected parties, the winner, and all those she is called to love and care for. Now, winning is not so much about an event or celebration as it is a culture and way of being. Winning is a rising tide that raises all boats.

A good winner may not make it to the podium for the ceremony. A winner isn't just someone who remains standing when the dust settles, but one who has invested into the network of players so that the game is played better because of the winner's time on the field. In this way of thinking, a good winner is the opposite of what I grew up thinking it was. A winner is not the father who has to apologize for his absence from home because of the time it took to build the empire. A winner is the coach who can build his empire out of his commitment to loving and investing in his family and community in a way that results in an effort to do without the best things in life.

Contrary to popular belief, a good winner doesn't have to lose connection with the ones they love to win. A good winner doesn't lose their spouse or their connection with their kids, hiding behind excuses like, *"I'm doing this for us."* One who can win well deliberately chooses long-term values over short-term victories. Every opportunity is a microcosm of the value-based life she chose at the beginning of the journey. A good winner fulfills commitments and is a woman of her word. She doesn't need to apologize for her absence because she establishes her time and energy investments based on the woman she knows she was created to become. Where others have excuses, she has resources and time to spare. Her priorities order her life. Anyone who would dare to apply these principles will begin to heal from their performance issues.

I wrote this chapter to reach several types of people. First, I wrote this to reach the person who lost themselves to satisfy someone else. I have shared how I was able to not only find myself again but also redefine the nature of my required performance in a way that was healthier for me, my audience, and those who would love me "off the stage." Demons that attach to the ego's need to shine will no longer haunt the healthy performer.

Secondly, I wrote this chapter to reach the person whose life performance was primarily motivated by a love of self. This shift in perspective will move your focus away from the person in the mirror to the mirror in all of us. No longer will your performance be burdened with the need for self-validation or praise.

Thirdly, I wrote this chapter to reach the performer who struggles with leaving the stage. A performer who has made the shift I made will be able to return to the always and ordinary without regret when the spotlight turns cold. In either case, the reader who sits with this chapter will be able to flow without effort, in truth and dignity. Not only will the "staged events" have more depth and authenticity, but the renewed performer will be refreshed for the offstage scenes where most of life occurs.

My father was a consummate performer. Though I attempted to apply his life standards in my life as brutally as he did, I now realize that the the effort to perform must be tempered with an awareness of how one moves in connection to everything and everyone else. In this second chapter, I am eager to talk about how the failure to temper performance with awareness can turn your best fruit into a poisonous tree.

I was born to win.

I have always known that. In every facet of human endeavor, I always competed, and I always won. I once believed that if I was winning, I must be doing what I was created to do. I also believed that when I lost, I had crossed the line and tread into an area outside of my destiny. Now I know what this is not the definition of winning at all. This is conforming. This is box-living. I lived this way for a great part of my life. Since I was praised for it, I thought I was doing something valuable.

How could I have been so wrong about something so fundamental to my identity? I always won because I played it safe. In this old version of myself, I loved the rules and considered myself the greatest at following directions. If a teacher told us to remain in our desks until she came back, you had better believe that no force known to man could have pulled me out of my chair. That is until I discovered a joy outside of the box.

I always saw myself as a model child. I knew I was *born to win*, but I played it so safe that nothing in my life reflected that belief. Because I had predetermined that I was the best at anything I would attempt, I would only attempt things I was extremely proficient at. I competed in math challenges because I was great at math. I signed up for track events because I was the fastest in my class (until Heather Wells moved to Huntsville).

At the bottom of my conformity was a fear of loss and rejection. I had predetermined that I would distinguish myself and discover my path by winning. I thought my wins would position me to be promoted or hired to be an institution's lead. I prized myself based on how much others esteemed me as better than they were. That meant everything to me.

I now know that you cannot win without taking risks. Winning begins with taking a deep dive into yourself to discover what you were uniquely created to bring to life. As you become willing to risk the trinkets of praise and the crumb-trappings of success, you begin to win. Winning has no meaning absent a result or prize. So, to consider the virtue of winning, one must pay attention to what they desire.

That's different for every person.

Winning for me may not be winning for you. This kind of definition of success is not transferable. It is like your fingerprints. You are the only one who has them.

I was so convinced that I had to win every task presented to me, there were times when I secretly broke the rules to get the win. I recall wanting an internship while in Auburn. They were down to the last two applicants. I was sitting in the lobby waiting to be interviewed when the other applicant came in. He looked like he had walked in straight from the cover of a Forbes magazine. The guy had to be Mark Zuckerberg's twin. *I had ranked higher than all of the other applicants, but how was I going to beat this guy?* I wondered.

During the interview, I did not admit that the idea to go to law school had not always been my vision (which was the story of Zuckerberg's twin who was coming in after me). I was there because I had a dream one night at the end of my junior year where I saw myself arguing a case in a courtroom. Instead of sharing my truth, I made up a background of all of the times in my life when I just knew I was going to practice law. It worked.

I was hired, but so was Zuckerberg.

As it turns out, he became a great friend and confidant that I had throughout law school. But this was not a win for me; this was an epic fail. I had not yet come to understand that winning by deception isn't winning at all. It sends you on a detour that will lead you someplace you were never supposed to be. You will be present in a life that was not your destiny, and the life designed for you will have escaped you. And people will be hurt along the way. *Just ask my ex-wife.*

Because I was determined to win in everything I competed in, I became willing to do anything to get the win. In so doing, I compromised every aspect of the character I thought I had. As if it did not matter, I would distract myself with the praise and glory of having won to cover up my shame for having lied or cheated my way into success.

Now, my standard for winning is directly tied to my destination. Every day that I come a step closer to where I was created to be is a winning day. On this side of deliverance, I am no longer everybody's favorite person. Before, I needed to be praised and celebrated at every moment, by every observer. Now, the kind of wins that I pursue often lead me away from the cheering crowd. I have little or no influence on the story that is told about what makes me tick.

One of the reasons I loved the crowd so much is that I was naturally drawn to those who had influence and voice, and I worked with them to write their narratives about me. So that even if I was not in the room, I knew exactly how I was talked about. I had reviewed their thoughts about me with them in private and rehearsed it so that whatever they said was filtered through the image I had of myself. I loved it because I had control of my narrative.

I couldn't see how much of a mess this tactic created in my life. If you had asked me, I would have said, *"Everything is amazing. My life is amazing."* Little did I know, my life was a disaster waiting to be discovered.

I was not the guy everybody thought I was. I was not innocent. I was not pure. I was not faithful. I was not gracious. I was not even loving. I loved on the condition that you played the game of life the same way I did, and if you were ever to discover any of my secret flaws, you were never to say anything about it. Under those conditions, you were gold in my book.

An even greater casualty of my need to control the narrative manifested when I began to neglect what my passions were telling me as it relates to new areas and new disciplines I needed to discover. Because I was determined to win everything, I wouldn't attempt anything hard or out of my comfort zone. I did not have time for any opportunity that required me to study, prepare, or pray.

It would take too much. Day after day and year after year, I drifted away from my path and began serving my interests instead of pursuing my transcendent destiny. I became a shell of myself.

All of the life, joy, and energy I had in abundant supply suddenly began to run low. I began to lose the excitement and pleasure I shared in my normal day-to-day course of life. It was like carrying sand in a bucket with a hole in it. But it was not just the fuel of my soul that began to spill — my body began to break down right along with it. Challenges and obstacles that I would leap over without thought became Olympic hurdles, and I was not trained for any of these events.

At various points in my journey, I have been a bad winner in three different ways. First, a bad winner is one who only competes in the areas of their strengths. I call this bad winner The Conformist. The most challenging aspect of evolving out of this evil is that most people probably have no idea they are doing anything self-defeating.

Secondly, a bad winner is one who needs to win for validation or acceptance. I was this guy too. Winning was not a natural result of alignment; it was a prerequisite for approval. I was loved because I was great at everything I did. This is also a very challenging perspective because I always thought, *"Well, this is what everybody else is doing. There cannot be anything wrong with it."* I call this bad winner The Perfectionist.

Thirdly, a bad winner is one who will win by any means necessary. This is the most obvious form of a bad winner. I call this guy The Determinist. This bad winner is probably the easiest to rescue. When giving an account of how they won, their evil should become obvious to them.

I had a friend in Boston who tried to intervene to help me with this years ago. Even though I could not hear what she was trying to say at that moment, I cannot forget her words. She said, *"Chauncey, what you don't realize is that everywhere you go, you leave a trail of bodies."* Eventually, I interpreted her words as an attempt to help me figure out how not to destroy the institutions I was trying to save. In actualizing my deliverance from being a bad winner, I had to become willing to lose often as I left paths that I was never supposed to be on in the first place.

I had to learn how to get comfortable submitting myself for a developmental process that may not result in a win. I had to come to the place where I was willing to break the rules to learn which ones aligned with my convictions. I was so used to being the favored one. I had to learn to become comfortable as the renegade, the rebel, and the person who would ask questions, challenge authority, and employ the process to engage as many people in the room in the win.

I learned that institutions that come from different cultural perspectives often have a very different definition of what it means to win. I had to become comfortable with pissing off people who had invited me into spaces that I otherwise would have never known existed. I had to accept that my access to the table was not solely about securing my wins but also securing the wins of those I love and care for.

Because everything in my life had been based on a public approval I no longer wanted, I had to replace that motivation with my approval. I had to write down what I was aiming for. I had to become comfortable returning home from work without having any boxes checked off on my shortlist of "Steps Needed to Win." I had to change my perspective on what it means to win and be invited to the race.

Now, before my days start, I spend time in my personal space. I repeat words of affirmation that reacquaint me with the path I have chosen and the man I am becoming. The most significant aspect of this personal time is the litany of gratefulness I have from the contacts and energies from the day before.

Originally, it started small with gratitude for things like money, gas, food, and transportation. Then, I moved to family, education, and experiences. Then, generational access to freedom and faith, through journeys of sharecropping parents, grandparents, and great-parents who were kidnapped, stolen, and forced to create wealth as fuel in oppressive economies. Then, suddenly, how I saw myself began to take on the universal significance of an important mountain range or river. I saw myself connected to this greater narrative that was not even about me.

It just included me, and that made me valuable to the scheme of redemption from the beginning of time until now.

After adopting a routine of gratitude practices, it became easy to stop competing with anybody for anything. I became comfortable with slowly developing a vision over time, then living out of that intention. Since I'm not competing with anyone, I share my destination with my friends and loved ones. I've discovered that I am not the only person who wants to see me evolve into my highest self.

Not only do I share my joys and successes, but I also share my fears and failures. The most liberating aspect of this lifestyle is that I am no longer living in isolation from everyone else around me. Before, I had this surface perfection. Now, I aim for deeper depths of truth and sincerity.

I have begun to attract a small group of friends interested in growing down instead of up. The investments of time and energy I make cause me to be more in tune and engaged rather than isolated and disconnected.

Finally, the satisfaction and joy I lost along the way have returned with passion to spare. Now, in meetings, I have to force myself to keep my voice down because the implications of our individual power to change our collective futures are so far-reaching, that we are scarcely able to fathom it. I challenge anyone reading this to apply a healthier standard of winning to every facet of life. Again, this is not a one-time event; this is a process. Good winning starts with good intentions tied to healthy values and a generous lifestyle. Once you adopt healthy winning perspectives, all of the people around you can become more relaxed with their standards and more connected to your journey as you will be to theirs.

You will be a winner who builds success through communal connections and doesn't need to apologize for missing out on the basic moves of life. When you purpose yourself to be available, you follow through on your commitments. You bring honor and integrity to every endeavor. You have energy and ideas to share. Your loved ones no longer slip through the cracks. A fragrance of gratitude will cover all your plans and retrospectives. When you reflect on the day that was or the day to come, you are renewed by your priorities of investment and no longer have to worry about spending more of your energy than you can collect. Your standards of grace and honor, receiving both good and bad reports, will become legendary.

You were born to win.

AFFIRMATIONS

I am endowed by a Supreme Power.

I am honored to live in this moment.

I am changing from what I regret to what I admire.

I am amazed to connect with today's dance of energy.

I am ready to accept all that I am.

I am made stronger by my courage.

CHAPTER THREE:

LOVING

I am a diamond in the rough, never again to be buried; for, I have been buried enough!

In Chapter Two, we discussed that a bad winner often only competes in the areas of their strengths to ensure their next victory. This narrow-minded approach has consequences, including a lack of holistic development. Everybody knows that if you want to become a better athlete, you don't just focus on the drills you are great at. You also focus on the weakest. The same is true when improving your quality of life.

We also learned that winning should not be based on the need to be accepted. Winning cannot be the source of our validation. When we strive to achieve with this mindset, validation and acceptance become our motivation for completing tasks.

Good winners aren't afraid to tackle those aspects of their characters that have not yet submitted to the process of transformation. Good winners move slowly. They are not hurried or out of time. Every move they make is consistent with their purpose. Whether or not they end up at the podium, their value is not determined by their outcome. They deserve the best that life has to offer, and they know it.

Finally, good winners are not primarily interested in their outcome; they invest in the outcomes of others. Their attitude and character allow those around them to expand. Many of our destinations are related and connected. Once we give up the solo act, we can truly become the collaborators the Creator Designer had in mind when she conceived us.

In this chapter, we will discuss how our personal relationships are connected to our pursuits and how easy it is to forsake our loved ones as we pursue what we deem are our just rewards. As we perfect our calling to love, we become infinitely closer to realizing success in this present realm and all others yet to come. I'll start by answering the question: What do you of when you hear the word *love*. I think of sacrifice. I think of someone emptying themselves to meet the needs of another.

If someone says they are good at loving, I interpret that to mean they are selfless and gracious, always considering others to be more important than themselves. The only time I have ever been referred to as a good lover was in regards to sex. In terms of relationship, I have never owned that title.

When I think of those who were good at loving me, I focus on family. That is not because I have not experienced love outside of my family, but because it is much easier for me to receive love from those who have full, working knowledge of who I am — the good, the bad, and the ugly.

What do I feel as I experience good love? I feel seen and

appreciated. I feel accepted and adored. I feel forgiven and redeemed. I feel honored and valued. Good love is born out of gratitude. It is as if God has moved through dimensions to arrive in the heart and body of one of his creations so that I perfectly know how he treasures me.

Being loved makes me feel safe.

My understanding of what love is has undergone a wild transformation, and as a result, I believe that love isn't sacrifice at all. Love is the least we can do to honor God in another person.

Being good in love now appears to require intention and attention.

Partly, I struggled with love because I feared being hurt or taken advantage of. Before my transformation, I would have considered myself often decent in love and occasionally good in love. However, I must acknowledge that of all the evils I have struggled with, love, by far, is the greatest. My failures in love are not the result of a lack of good models. I am now utterly speechless when I consider how privileged I am to have had the opportunity to learn love from such amazing teachers.

My parents and siblings have loved me and each other well, but my father has to win the award. Every member of my family would agree that his love for his children was biblical. It was unlike anything I'd ever seen.

If my dad was Abraham, I was Isaac. I made sure of that.

I made myself the son of promise. I set my mind to accomplish everything my father did, and then some. He was all for it.

He set me up to conquer the world. Later, I would have to reconcile my identity, the life I had lived through the eyes of my father, while on my sickbed. But as clear as I was about who he was and what made him tick, that's how unclear I was about who I was. I never needed to define myself while he was alive. He was great, and I was his son.

His love made me safe.

It secured me. I remember as a kid having to go to bed before he got home. I would just lay there and not even begin to fall asleep. When I heard his car pull up in the driveway and his key turn the lock, I could rest.

The first time I was convinced of the power that love could play in my life was when I moved into my first apartment. I was so excited. I had been living with my brother since before I pledged our fraternity. Then, I moved to the Goodwin Apartments. Recco, who was one of my best friends at the time, knocked on the door a few minutes after I unpacked my stuff and noticed that I forgot to bring food from my old place. The last time I had heard the words, *"Hold out your hand,"* was one of the many times in my childhood when I was about to be palm-slapped by my heavy-handed father for disappointing him. But, on this occasion, I suspiciously obliged the request.

I held out my left hand, and he opened his hand over mine. One hundred and thirty-seven dollars in food stamps fell through my hand and to the floor.

When I asked what it was for, he said he had collected an offering from his family up the street. Outside of my family, his brother Eric had been the first to show me love. I never got used to it. The ease with which they were able to show me love was completely foreign. I had so much to learn.

What I learned from my fraternity brothers slowly began to change my life and create within me the capacity to extend myself on behalf of others. It had never crossed my mind how everything I had ever done before college had been all about me.

Loving takes me outside of myself. It gives me eyes to see the experience and needs of others. Loving makes me want to share whatever I have, in whatever way it may be useful. I tried to use the love I had for my brothers in Auburn to replace my inability to love myself. I never believed I deserved love because I felt I hadn't earned it yet. I remember trying to give the food stamps back to Recco. There was no way I could take something of that great value. Surely, if I were more transparent, I wouldn't even have had the opportunity to say no.

Even when I proposed to and married my on-and-off-again girlfriend, I expected at any moment I'd be exposed. I hadn't earned love yet. I was still deeply in the rough. I was not good enough, strong enough, or worthy enough, and it became a self-fulfilling prophecy.

The conflict for me now comes from the fact that as great a model as I had, I am not sure my father ever knew how much I loved him. He often said he never expected me or my siblings to be there when he could no longer live in his home. Decades before his senior years, he would regularly recite to his church members, *"I'm not expecting anybody to be there for me when that time comes.*" I knew he was wrong in his assessment, but it bothered me that he held this conviction.

I always appreciated being my father's son because he never failed to let me know what he thought about me. My dad did not buy me a card for my sixteenth birthday; he wrote me a poem. Now, I'm a good writer, but my father was legendary. It's still hard to believe that he was never published. The poem my father wrote to me is one of my most valuable gifts. It was entitled "A Diamond In The Rough."

I had never heard that expression before, so I was somewhat at a loss to catch the point. It read, *"Son, you're rough around the edges. But you will be great one day."* One day? I thought. Most people think I'm great now, don't they? Actually, they did not. But I did not realize it until much later.

If I was engaging with people on a surface level, it was very easy for me to show love to them. The closer people got to me, the more difficult showing love became. By the time I got to those closest to me, I expected them to just know I loved them. I felt like I did not have to express it because I had been expressing love all day, everywhere else. At home, everybody should just know. It probably dawned on me to buy a poster that said, *"Oh, by the way, y'all already know I love you, so don't expect me to ever do or say anything to prove it."*

Even worse than my lack of intention or energy for expressing love where it counted most was the expectation I had to be loved by those very same people. I was completely ignorant about how these relationships were supposed to work. I just assumed that if you were close enough to me to see the greatness I was aiming for, you should ask me how you could help me love the world. You should make some kind of offer to support my endeavor. I can't do this by myself, can I?

So when I was around, I expected the attention to be on me. It did not matter who else was there or what else was going on. I expected some continual acknowledgment of the sheer volume of work I was doing to be great in the world. There was no amount of attention that was too much. It all paled in comparison to the amount of attention I felt I deserved.

To say that I was greedy in my relationships is putting it mildly. I could have starred in Seven Deadly Sins as myself. I had the most evil expectations around love. My problem was not that I was ungrateful for my family and those who dared to love me. If any one of them had accused me of lacking in love for them, I would have completely broken down in disbelief. I had a world of gratitude for each of them, but I did not have a voice to express it. I was completely oblivious about it until I got married.

Love is natural. Love is simple. Love is easy. I had heard all of this my whole life. As ridiculous as it sounds to me now, I fell for it. There was no way that I ever considered that I had to be intentional in order to show love. Private love was never easy for me, but public expressions were. I could get in front of a group of people and express hope, belief, and possibility, all day long. I guess I figured that my loved ones had been present on so many of those occasions, they certainly had to know I loved them. Expressing it privately would be redundant, no?

The origin of my struggle with love comes from being the middle child of three kids. In college, I heard of the middle child syndrome and knew instantly that they were talking about me. Due to the level of awareness I had at that time, I was only capable of hearing the good part. I knew that middle children were overachievers because they felt neglected and overlooked. I took that to explain my obsession with accomplishment and perfection. It made sense. And in fact, it was not my fault. It was because of my birth order.

If they had wanted me to be different than I was, they should have had me in better order. I thought. *Who wants to be in the middle, anyway?* The middle of anything is always suspect. The middle of the movie is the worst part. The middle of a story makes you fall asleep. In the middle of a song, your mind starts to wander. The middle seat on a plane? Exasperating! I even slept in a bedroom in the middle of the house. Every morning, I woke up over it already. Everybody walked through my room on their way from one important place to another, and they would d leave both of my doors open. *Clearly, I'm still not over it.*

What I could not appreciate was the motivation behind the achievement and its relationship to inferiority. I did not realize that I lost my status when my younger sibling was born. I was no longer special. Every day since, I've felt that everybody owed me a debt for taking something away that was mine — my attention, my role, my purpose, and my uniqueness.

And so, at the age of five, I went on a mission to earn my way back into relevance. I planned to show them and the world that they had slept on the wrong one. I started working on a plan to become the most significant person in the history of my community. I would perform, write, sing, speak, dance, and study. I would become. I would inspire.

And that's exactly what I did. All because I lost my place.

Now what is crazier than everything I have shared so far is the fact that this entire victim narrative was entirely my creation. I developed a regular response that I relied on in my childhood home, but it followed me first to undergrad, then to law school, and then into the workforce. I always competed for attention. I always strategized to see how I could pull attention from someone else to make situations more about me.

In all of my relationships, I expected those around me to just know I had to love them; it was not like I was without other options. I told myself that I deserved whatever came and that whatever went was never for me. I now know that I was copping out. I was fully prepared to accept the victim's status, but I never considered my responsibility to manage my wellness process.

What makes a person bad in loving? There are three things that may make a person bad in love. First, you can fail to have love in your heart for another person. This is the most fundamental evil and the least familiar to me. I have never struggled to love people who were contributing to my life.

The second evil in love is the most familiar to me. It is the failure to demonstrate love to the people who need to see it most. As I have mentioned, this is where I can grow the most. I now use a significant portion of every conversation I have with family and friends to remind me just how much I appreciate them sharing who they are with me and apologizing for having taken it for granted in years past.

The third evil in love may be the most insidious but the easiest for me to rectify. It is the feeling that while someone may be naturally lovable, they have no right to my expression of love until they do something sacrificial. My problem in this area results from the transference of my need to achieve a lovable status. This incidental evil resulted from a feeling of inadequacy on my part. I thought I had to perform to be worthy of love. In the process of healing from this ridiculous philosophy, my perspective on love has matured, and my mishaps in love have naturally restored. I learned that love is not a natural fragrance that people close to you can just automatically experience and receive. Love is an intention. It is an effort.

My failure in love was also about a lack of desire to invest energy in communication. I preferred to spend energy on myself instead of others. This did not make me special; it made me less than ordinary. The kind of love I know I am capable of is extraordinary. The kind of love I believe makes the most sense also requires the most work. I was not willing to do that work.

I no longer excuse my failures in love as the necessary costs of greatness. I remind myself of the kind of expressions I would love to hear if I were in my loved ones' shoes, and I speak to those issues when I communicate with them. I start by reminding myself that the love that I have always experienced was not attributable to my talents or achievement but to my creation in the image of God.

When someone else loves me, it is because they connect with

the divinity inside of me, and that is my intention as I meet and reacquaint myself with others.

I celebrate God in everyone. I practice as I observe crowds walking in shopping areas or sporting events. I ask myself, *"Do you see God in her, in him, in them? Are you prepared to engage with them with equal interest and concern as you would want them to engage with you? Do you lovingly engage because you believe the best of them, or are you turning this engagement into another task you will later be proud of?"*

I am retraining myself to have one encounter at a time. It is having a huge impact on the possibilities of every interaction. I am being invited to share space and time with so many people in different areas. I trust that what I will learn about them will make my interest in engaging with them even stronger. And it has become a self-fulfilling prophecy. I am truly grateful for it.

I am cautious to consider myself suddenly on the other side of my deliverance process in this area. I am aware that I will probably struggle in this area for some time because I turned my vice into virtue.

With my family and closest friends, I can own my previous difficulties. I can share how hard I have struggled in this area and how excited I am to work through my failure in community. I also share my conviction that I believe love is something that has to be worked out through relationships and how excited I am to believe that one day, I will have the opportunity to love intimately and graciously as I know I was created to.

Finally, I am cautiously optimistic, as I begin to meet old

friends in a new light, that I will be able to ask for and receive forgiveness for the many times I allowed my greed to stand in the way of my love.

Anyone who would dare to apply these principles will be reminded of how it felt to be loved without restraint. Once this memory fully returns, worth and acceptance will soon follow. These traits follow the life of someone who lives in a place of gratitude. You cannot love what you do not appreciate.

Whereas before you accepted this challenge, you may have seen the act of love as a call to biblical sacrifice reserved for the noblest of heroes who can look pasts others' faults and see their needs. You will now see the commitment to love as a reasonable service for someone who is as grateful as you are.

One of the consequences of love that no transformation can change is the risk of being hurt. This risk is inherent in the nature of love itself. And thank God for that. I think we would all be more grateful for these risks if we could be reminded how often these risks were ignored as our friends and loved ones attempted to love on us.

When we love with intention and purpose, we make those around us feel safe. When we give of what we have, even when it is in short supply, we communicate that all around us, there are more than enough resources to go around at any given moment. Love is one of the greatest stretch exercises you can ever attempt. It will tone your muscles and heal your heart. Love can move you from the depths of hopelessness to the hills of triumph, with no change in circumstance. Don't be stingy with it. Give love away.

AFFIRMATIONS

I am blissful with awareness.

I am connected to my vibration.

I am not distracted by my imperfections.

I am honored to discover my truth.

I am made stronger by everything manifesting through me.

I am aware of my spiritual experience.

CHAPTER FOUR:
CHOOSING

God doesn't make rich people or poor people. God makes people.

Myles Munroe

In the last chapter, I shared how love moves you beyond the surface into the depths of the heart. I had to grow to the point where showing love did not feel like a weakness but instead a strength. Previously, I lacked intention and reserved expressions of love for people who never needed to hear it from me. I just assumed that everyone else knew how I felt.

As a result of my transformation, I know how simple it is to commit to love. The act remains challenging, but the work flows from the commitment, heart connection, and recognizing that someone else's journey is yours to assist with. As you assist them, they assist you. This was particularly tough for me to learn because I had always connected love with performance. I felt loved because of what I could do, so I expected anyone who needed love from me to do the same. The bad habits of expressing love that I learned as a kid followed me throughout my life and almost robbed me of my chances of ever finding a healthy love language. I am so grateful that those around me were patient enough to remain invested in my journey, even while I was absent from theirs. The struggle with love that was toughest for me was not global or communal; it was personal. If I knew you at a surface level, I would completely engage, but if you were my loved one, I did not see the point.

The principles in the last chapter demonstrate how a healthy practice of love not only changes the life experience of everyone around you, it changes you at a quantum level. You no longer see everyone as isolated units of matter. If they don't matter, neither do you. Love beckons. Love calls you home. Once you sit in that place, you will never move again.

In this chapter, we will discuss how a lack of intention doesn't just affect relationships; it affects outcomes. In so many areas of my life, better results were at my fingertips. I just did not choose to experience them. As I begin to identify with my failures, opportunities to experience the return on greater investments of energy always eluded me, and I was bitter about it. Learning to accept responsibility for my choices has more power to affect my outcomes than almost any other phenomenon on earth. So now, I'm choosing my best outcomes, starting with wealth.

When I hear the word *choice*, I think of luxury. If someone is choosing, they have multiple options available. The one who is choosing is aware of their access and is comfortable with deciding which option goes best with their sense of self. Although I recognize many of the privileges I had growing up, I am largely frustrated when I consider the possibility that more opportunities for success were awaiting me had I known to choose them. When I hear about someone choosing success, I feel mocked. Although I have had my share of success, I've also seen many failures. Some of them are harder to get past than others, particularly public failures and failures in areas where I thought success was my birthright.

Accepting responsibility was never my strength. I had difficulty realizing the good choices available because of my reluctance to accept responsibility for my bad choices. It was much easier for me to blame someone or something else. I avoided the negative feelings of having a choice. I added insult to that injury by claiming a right to empathy or even sympathy for not being dealt a better hand.

Before the change in mindset that led to me writing this book, no one could have convinced me that I could have chosen to be more successful than I was. *Who would fail to choose a better life?* If I had been aware of the choices I failed to make that resulted in me struggling to pay my bills, my anxiety for not having more of the trappings of success would be much greater. Rather than consider the alternative, I created a reality that masked my personal responsibility.

The last time I was able to save was in New York when they took out my retirement before I saw it. I have not saved anything I have seen. For most of my life, I have been financially embarrassed. I avoided one of the most important principles of life: management. The key to good management is good stewardship, effective delegation, and distribution of resources. That is what good managers do. Rather than being bothered with the obvious consequences of my failure to plan, I chose to believe my emotions would move God. I felt like God saw me struggling, knew I loved him, and that everything I did was for him. I believed he wouldn't allow me to miss bill payments and that at any moment, my blessing would be on the way.

Maybe I thought that if I could just get God to feel sorry for me, I could get anything I wanted. As I think about it, I wanted to have my cake and eat it too. I felt like I could spend money the way I wanted and still have money to do whatever I needed to do. *But who has ever lived like that?* Nobody, that's who. God is going to "make up the difference."

I wished.

Had God responded to me like that, how would I have ever come to understand who he is and what he created me for. God loves me so much that he directs, but he doesn't demand. God wants me to spend my life using my faculties to figure some of this stuff out. The story of my life, as it relates to success and profits, was one of few highs and many lows. Worrying about whether or not I could ever buy a home, afford to get married, or pay off my student loans was the most consistent emotion of my life.

In the course of my worrying, I did some of the craziest things imaginable. I spent everything I made. In a few seasons, I spent much more than I made. Of course, that brought incredible debt into my life. Debt for me was not only physical or financial; it took on an emotional and spiritual weight. It became an ever-present awareness of what was unavailable for me. It was a constant affirmation of what I was not entitled to and a constant reminder of what I did not deserve.

I never considered it my opportunity to save or invest. I never had any financial margin. Whereas my initial assessment of lack may have been a product of my imagination, my failure to choose a better outcome made that image a reality. This never-ending cycle repeated so often that I believed that poverty was my destiny and my curse was to forever chase what I would never capture.

I preferred to see my lack of growth as some kind of spiritual testing designed to weed out those less faithful than Job and me. I considered my lack of growth as some kind of spiritual wager result that had nothing to do with me. I allowed myself to think that if I was not so righteous, I could do those dirty, underhanded, sneaky things that businessmen do to build fortunes. But the path of righteousness requires sacrifice and the monastic life. I held close to my heart a theology that allowed me to credit the supernatural for what I could not accomplish in the physical. I saw my lack of success as a "reward" for my righteousness. God was testing me.

I could never support my theology with a prominent story from the Bible. It does not even make common sense, but that did not stop me from believing it. Consistent with my pie-in-the-sky theology, God was either going to wait until he found me faithful enough to trust me with more, or he was going to reward me in heaven. After all, I did not want to make the mistake of receiving my riches on earth and risking having nothing waiting for me in eternity, did I?

Poppycock! Yeah, I said it. Genesis indicted my foolish thinking. According to this narrative and consistent with common sense and sound management principles, I never saw increase, savings, or wealth because of my faithfulness, but my lack thereof. We have all heard it said that he who is faithful over a few things will become ruler over many. So at a very basic level, had I put myself in the position to manage growth, growth would have come. Had I put myself in the position to become faithful over the few dollars I had, God would have trusted me with more.

My theology allowed me to blame God for my lack of success. *How ironic is that?* I made the same mistake so many people make today. I held God responsible for what I was not willing to invest. I fell into the obvious trap of making God prove himself to me. And not only that, I was vocal about it. If someone asked me, I would have implicated my belief structure to justify my lack of wealth.

Perish the thought.

The idea is old as dirt but as ridiculous now as it has ever been. God doesn't make rich people or poor people. He just makes people. God doesn't care who manages the land, as long as someone does. If I continually blame him for my failure to position myself for success, I continue the cycle of victimization and blaming other people for what I refuse to do. I have recently come to believe that I may not have ever had the money problem I embraced. I had a self-control problem. I had a contentment problem and several discipline problems. At the root, my problem was spiritual.

My anxiety was strong evidence of the errors in my belief. I placed my faith in temporary tangibles rather than the eternal incorruptible. I saw myself as someone who borrowed but never lent, rented but never owned, leased but never bought. Everything I owned or did not own was about me and my worth. Whatever I possessed or controlled was the commentary on how favored, excellent, or loved I was. My success was all about me.

Instead of being gracious and generous, I had been greedy. There is no better way to say it. I did the same thing with wealth as I had done with love. I never chose to be generous. It just dawned on me. When I reflected on myself, I realized my problem was fundamental. I believed wealth should just come to me because I deserved it. After all, the riches of the wicked are laid up for the righteous or something King James said like that, right? *Nah. Not even close.*

Greed is the management of resources for personal benefit. A greedy spirit will manipulate resources. I figured out a way to be the ultimate beneficiary of everything I did. *Win-win.* If the Son of Man is right, and my financial life demonstrates that he is, greed will destroy. My greed came from my arrogance. I thought I was better than everybody else. In the process of attempting to distinguish myself, I defined myself. While hoping to show the world that whatsoever a man soweth that shall he also reap, I confessed my evil by being regularly broke.

It is embarrassing that it took me so long to learn that basic lesson. There I was, thinking that I was setting myself apart from some greater calling. I was setting myself up for failure. Again and again and again. Then, I created a narrative to justify it. *It's not my fault. It's systemic. A black man in America can't get ahead. Because for every payment he makes, there are two he owes. So, I just won't make any payments.*

What good will it do, anyway? I lose anyway. That is what we do as black people in America — we lose. And we don't lose small; we lose big. We lose fabulously. We lose gloriously. They make memes about our losses, and they all go viral. The cost of my never-ending pursuit for a bigger and better life created a growing hole inside my soul. Once I moved out of my parents' house into an apartment, I immediately started thinking of the days when I could rent a bigger place and then own my first home. Even with this emphasis, it took me twenty years before I bought my first car.

Living in discontent and boxing myself as a consumer made me believe that the best in life was not available. But as I thought about generosity, the first image that came to mind were the gifts that many black celebrities make to HBCUs. Oprah gives 25 million. Lebron James gives 15 million. *Once I get that money, I'm gonna be generous like that.* I thought. But in actuality, that is not what the research suggested. Hell, I did not need to consult a study to know that. I could just look at my account history. No matter the deposit, it was almost gone before I got my next check. Discouraged and despondent, I abandoned my hopes of ever being generous. I just hadn't been dealt those cards. I believed that I would be poor. Even Jesus said, *"The poor will always be with you."* I had always thought that he was talking TO me, but I never realized that he was talking ABOUT me.

The idea of a plan seemed antithetical to my creative personality. *Why should I have to plan? If I decide to be generous, should not it just flow naturally?* Actually no.

My lifestyle had created a financial plan for me, but I was not aware of it. *But, why not?* Had I not been paying attention to the repeated overdrawn checking account emails I got every day? No. I was not aware of it because I chose not to be. I lived in denial. I knew that if I ever accepted my poor planning and management skills, I would have to do something about it. To avoid the work, I took the easy way out and chose to turn a blind eye.

It's not me; it's them.

Because I did not know my plan, I discovered that I had a bad plan — a plan that operated outside of my value system. I was operating a plan that I was not responsible or accountable for. I constantly positioned myself to need a financial miracle from God. *"Do it, God. I know you can. You see my faults, God. I need you to 'make up the difference.'"*

So how did I just so easily pass my responsibility for managing my resources on to God? Why was I so comfortable depending on God to do for me financially what I would never ask him to do in any other area of my life? If I needed to learn a song or give a speech, I wouldn't pray in front of my computer. I would download the song and learn it. I would open a book and study. I had never been spiritually lazy about anything else. But somehow, I made this exception for wealth. God, I know you want me to have a house because you own the cattle on a thousand hills. Do it, God. I know you can. Whenever I wanted something, I planned for it. Whenever I did not care, I prayed for a miracle.

Since I began this work of deliverance, I think very differently about what comes through my hands. I no longer subscribe to the thought that whatever comes to me is for me.

Much of what was given to me was not for me to ever own. As it relates to resources, my role is not as much about what I can receive as it is about what I can give.

Assuming that every success I found was about me and that every dollar I made was mine to spend caused me to place my value in things rather than my character. This ideology allowed me to be content as a consumer without any greater vision of what it meant to earn and live. I believe God had something else in mind when he breathed into my nostrils and made me a living soul.

I am in the process of breaking my cycle of discontentment by reordering my life around generosity. The more I sit with myself and meditate on my value, I have determined that everything I own is given for me to share. At this point, the challenge was figuring out how to be generous when I am struggling to survive. *How can I give away what I do not have? Wouldn't it make more sense for those with much to share their resources with those of us who have so little?*

I discovered that destiny for poverty makes no sense. This idea is so popular but is impossible if what we say we believe about the abundance in the universe is true. There is no way that God designed some of us to be rich and others of us to be poor. He couldn't do that and love us all at the same time. That would make him too much like us. Maybe I preferred my nature in heaven instead of God's. That way, I could blame him for what I had not accomplished. However, my preference would make Him someone other than who he is.

When I order my life from a place of generosity instead of poverty, I release what never belonged to me in the first place.

I thought that to be generous, I had to be spontaneous, but I needed to be a good manager. I needed to decide what I would do with my success before it came so that I could have the life I chose.

I believe God meant it when he said, *"Be fruitful and multiply."* I believe God created us to dominate the earth. But I created a loophole for myself that allowed me an exemption from doing the work everyone else was called to do. I wasted so many resources; it is a shame.

God did not create me to become the best performer on the national stage; he did not need another actor or singer. God has millions of musicians on every continent. But what he did not have was millions of good managers.

The concepts in this chapter have moved me far from blaming others for my lack of success. It has never been anybody's fault but mine. I hate it, but it is true. I wish I had a fraction of the energy I spent being frustrated and upset at everyone for not giving me a better life. I could power a small city for a year. The principles I've shared in this chapter helped me realize that debt does not belong to me; I just haven't been able to let it go. It defined my life for so long that I forgot who I was without it.

Reading this chapter will give you many reasons to reconsider whose faithfulness is implicated by your lack of success. I discovered it was mine. Now, I am comfortable admitting my ineptness and have put myself in a better position to be excellent in management.

The reader who applies the principles in this chapter will stop praying to win the lottery or receive a $50,000 check in the mail. Instead, he will pray to become a good steward of the small stream of income that has consistently trickled down. Then, and only then, will that trickle become a stream and that stream a river. If you apply these principles regarding healthy choices, you will quickly discover that you were never fated to lose. God has not cursed your life, your family, or your community. Instead, God reserves growth for those with the vision to manage it.

AFFIRMATIONS

I am endowed with absolute potential.

I am filled with security and truth.

I am connected to my perfect path.

I am free to choose my outcome.

I am grateful for my journey.

I am motivated by my process.

CHAPTER FIVE:
LETTING GO

Last night I lost the world, and gained the universe.

C. JoyBell C.

In the last chapter, I shared my previous notice that choosing was a luxury. I shared that we all have a choice. And when we fail to choose abundance, we choose lack. Even though I had many privileges as a kid, I began to accept a destiny of scarcity that never belonged to me. What's worse, I blamed that destiny on a God who failed to "bless" me with abundance, undermining my faith and witness. But now, I no longer run from my past. Although it has been full of disappointments, hurts, and a few big wins, I embrace it all.

Every event in my life has more to teach me. I am sure I learned more from my losses than from my wins. I now accept responsibility for all that has happened. It couldn't have happened that way for anyone else. It is my choice to embrace what it came to teach me and make myself a better man.

I will conclude the story of my transformation by discussing the challenge I have had with letting go. It seems a natural finale to the path I have undertaken, and the concept itself may be the scariest of all.

When I hear the term *letting go*, I think of a parent who has to bury a child who was murdered by a police officer. I think of a boy in a hospital who just found out that his stage 4 cancer has returned. I think of the New England Patriots trailing by 21 and the opposition celebrating on the field. For most my life, I thought of someone who deserved to be in their current position but were robbed of their next victory for reasons beyond their control. Now, I think of someone with an unhealthy attachment who has to let go in order to embrace their best life.

Letting go is not about justice or fairness. It is about wellness. When you carry around old weights and old disappointments, you are not flexible or nimble. You are heavy. And everyone who attempts to partner with you has to share the load. Letting go of the old hurt or original goals is not as much about a ceremony or a final adjudication. It's about reorienting from the shaded past to a shining future.

One who can let go for the better has become an expert in healing. She is learning to balance commitments and expectations safely and naturally. She does not get thrown off by what does not follow her lead. She is able to go with the flow, wherever it leads. She is not intimidated by what she has not learned. She is eager to apprentice at the feet of the hidden artist whose masterpiece has yet to be revealed. She knows that change is the natural movement of life. And in her due seasons, she releases old objectives and agendas just as a tree releases dead leaves.

Contrary to popular belief, the one who lets go for the better does not have to release alone. When she lets go of her old infatuations and loves, her heart opens, and space is made for new friends, acquaintances, and lovers to share the joys and pains of a life with no end in sight. Letting go is not for the faint at heart. This moment is reserved for the truly strong and courageous. Not content to see herself any longer through old near-sighted eyes, her perception has been taken out 50,000 feet above the earth.

She doesn't just observe her path; she understands it.

One of the hardest things for me to do was to relax. When I was not working on finishing my next project, I grieved the previous project that I had not finished and planned the next project. I didn't understand how others just stopped when they finished work, and they are just done for the day. I had never been that guy. I was nothing if not a machine.

I preferred to stay engaged until I went to sleep. When I dreamed at night, I would fantasize about my next engagement. Then, when I woke up, it started over again.

I was always evaluating myself based on my last failure. I tried to dot every preparatory *i* and cross every thoughtful *t*. If you were to walk past me on the street, you wouldn't have noticed me. I worked hard to blend in. Nothing about my physical appearance had ever been impressive. But when I started to speak and move, drama flowed from every pore, and I would have your undivided attention.

I am the definition of an underdog. I love to be underestimated.

It is my favorite way to enter a room. Now that my young adult life is ending and middle age is approaching, I have a heightened sense of the drama in my philosophy and personal life. As a result of my recent transformation, I have an increased awareness of what it means to be alive.

What it meant and what it will mean.

One of the greatest hindrances to my happiness was the weight of past disappointments and failures. I took too much responsibility for not only what I did but how everyone responded. And with each new endeavor, I spent far too much time attempting to control my outcome by predetermining how others react to me. It became too much for me to handle. I trace this practice back to May 1993 when I was graduating from college.

It was an amazing time. I was about to become the first of my siblings to get a college degree. I had been numb throughout my engineering curriculum. There were classes I enjoyed, but for the most part, I knew I was pledging an academic fraternity I never wanted to become identified with. The only reason I chose it was because it took almost no effort for me. In college, I was excited about discovering community.

I had fallen in love with the residents of Lee County. I was completely enamored with them, and they were with me. I had been adopted into several families and thought I would never know love like that again. Graduating meant that all of that was about to come to an end. I did not want to leave, but apparently, I had to go and become something.

During my senior year, I took one required class, and the rest were electives. This class was Power. I loved the concept of the class but hated the professor — Charles Gross. He did not like me. He did not think I deserved to be in that class. At my college, there were very few black students. Those who were there were quiet and unassuming. Most students who wanted to study engineering were intimidated by the curriculum. I never paid it any attention. And then, one day, in the middle of that semester, the professor read out the names of the graduating seniors because their grades had an earlier due date. When he read my name, he looked around the room. He had no idea who I was. From that point, he did everything he could to prevent me from passing his class.

I went to his office after class several times. He glossed over the material and did not explain how we should solve the problems. I would stand in line outside his office like several other students who needed the class to graduate. When it was my time to enter, he would never make eye contact with me. Without looking up, he would say, "I covered that in class. Weren't you paying attention?" I assured him that I had paid attention, and he did not cover it; he glossed over it. Other students had answer keys to many of the exams in their dorms. Very few black students had even taken Power at the time, so our fraternity did not have this class on file. Needless to say, I did not do very well on the final.

I sent graduation invitations all the same. While my family was in town, I discovered that I had not passed his class and would not graduate that semester. This was the first time in my life I had ever missed a mark I invested in. I was disoriented. It was probably the first time I had ever considered committing suicide. Who was I if not the person who finished their bachelor's in four years? Who was I, if not my father's engineering graduate? What the hell was I supposed to do?

To add insult to injury, I had already been accepted to law school in the fall, and I was attending an urban missionary event with Campus Crusade for Christ in South Central Los Angeles. I had to make a choice. I could have stayed for the summer, missed the mission trip, and still enrolled in law school in the fall, or I could leave for the summer, go on the mission trip, defer my law school entrance a year, and return in the fall to complete my degree.

I chose the second option.

Even though this all worked out in my favor, this was the day I realized I had a serious problem with attachments. Failing my first class in life should not have impacted how I felt about myself as a person, but it did. It was the first of many failures in performance, competitions, relationships, and money management. Surrendering my original graduation plan in favor of a second plan that was not as rigid, tight, or supernatural was the best thing I could have ever done.

My mental orientation is high in perception and insight. These two attributes convinced me that I was infallible and made me over critical of myself and everyone around me. As a result, the attitudes of those around me were far more important to me than they should have ever been. This undermined my confidence in many ways. Those who have attempted to be close to me in this process have often been hurt. All I can ever do is ask for their forgiveness and turn over a new leaf.

Letting go is not a completely foreign idea for me. Previously, if I got to the point of letting go, it was not for the better, but the worse. Firstly, when I let go before, it was out of anger and resentment. When someone I collaborated with repeatedly failed to follow through, I was forced to let go of my expectations that any new possibilities would ever emerge.

Secondly, there are scores of relationships, personal and professional, that I have let go of prematurely. Because I was juggling so many commitments simultaneously, I forced them to compete with each other. Only those colleagues who were able to keep up with me got to run alongside. I would let the others go.

Thirdly, letting go is my response to being already rejected. It is what I do when I have been a disappointment to someone else, been abandoned, blocked, or ghosted. It has sometimes taken me months to remove a ghosted friend from my contacts list.

Since 1993, I have been tied to an old anchor that weighs heavier with each new opportunity. This anchor has grown with every new thought, worry, and fear from the past and even about the future. This anchor has held me back from the light of freedom I was created to inhabit. I have missed so many intended synchronicities and appointments. I have cheated myself out of so many joys and breakthroughs because I would not break away from the anchor that secured me. Faced with the possibility of being forever bound to my past or finally released into my future, I had a choice to make. I could continue to drag my anchor over hills and into valleys, like the ghost of Christmas past, or I could find a way to escape the tie and soar. *How did I begin the process of overcoming my evil in letting go?* I would love to say that I was able to pull away from the weight of old disappointments and immediately take flight. But I didn't bind myself in a day, and it took quite an investment to be rid of the old, lesser version of me. My therapist taught me that when I attach as quickly and as deeply as I do, that is symptomatic of a truly addictive personality. My unduly deep attachments resulted in debilitating dependencies and breakups so painful that they resembled drug withdrawals.

To begin my growth, I had to structure my relationships so that everyone had their own space and was able to live and develop on their terms. Instead of running away from my tendency to attach too deeply, I often bring the image back to my mind, and I sit with it. I see myself on a beach on the edge of the shore. My toes are hot with the heat of the sand, and the tops of my feet are wet with the undulating tide. Out in the sea, I see my canoe I want to grace, and just as I begin to make my way out into the water, I feel a tug around my waist. I turn around and see a rusty iron anchor, partially buried deep into the sand. I sit down on the edge of the shore into the water.

Instead of focusing on the anchor, I focus on the canoe and imagine the salt in the ocean taking on a supernatural power that can dissolve the rope's fabric. I do not sit there for long. I do not want to belittle my process. After weeks and then months, the fabric begins showing wear.

This practice goes against my nature and personality. Before the days of my higher consciousness, if I saw something I wanted out of my reach, I did everything in my power to pursue it with all deliberate speed.

I would have been looking for a knife, sword, or piece of glass on the beach. I would have cut my hands or bruised my ribs, abusing my body for the sake of pulling the rope. Rather than fight against nature, I no longer pull. I sit. I make myself content to be in process and participate in an everyday practice that liberates me slowly — *one-hundredth of a strand of rope at a time.*

If you could have seen a graph of the energy I spent each day before my conversion, it would have looked like a flat line at the highest decibel. Now, the shape of the energy I spend each day looks like a mountain. It begins with my calendar. I try to only have one important event each day instead of the four I used to schedule.

Secondly, I set my alarm at night to wake me up two hours before I need to leave the house. Thirdly, when I wake up, I move very slowly. I take my time progressing through a morning routine that includes meditations, affirmations, prayers, and check-ins with my loved ones, in-person and online. Once my day ends, I have slowed my pace to a crawl. I return to my bed with affirmations and check-ins.

I am not as busy. In fact, I'm not busy at all. But I am fulfilled. I don't value the success of my days based on how many people I saw or how many meetings I had. I value my days by how present, available, and attentive I was to the opportunities that presented themselves to me. *Did I recognize the Godly spark in the eyes of people I spoke with? Was I interested in their journey, or did I view them as mere supporting actors in my leading role?* My whole life has changed. Instead of feeling stressed and anxious in every waking moment, I feel calm and balanced. This sense of balance is not only growing inside me; it is also spreading to those I love, talk to, and see daily. I feel like I have taken control of my mind. I am most conscious of this when things that would ordinarily trigger me come into my view and then immediately drift away as if I never saw them.

Instead of the isolation I had grown accustomed to, I feel connected around me and express concern for everyone. I feel invested in the lives and journeys of those around me. I want to be the best investor in their success and constantly remind them to take advantage of my resources. I believe that whatever I experience in life, be it fantastic or devastating, I am not the sum total of my experiences. I am bigger than that. I am connected to the whole.

Marchadangel says, *"You may not be responsible for everything that happened to you when you were younger, but you need to be responsible for undoing the thinking patterns these circumstances created. Blaming your past for a limiting mindset does not fix it. Change your response to what you remember."* By yielding to nature's call for my latest transformation, I am developing the skills to create conditions for sustainable happiness. I don't associate my good feelings with my accomplishments or with any pleasure, emotion, or mood —all of that is fleeting. What I am discovering now is a joyful state of being. *Imagine that for a Type-A personality like mine.* I am finally finding success and balance by being healthy and breathing in and out attentively and intentionally each day. Not only that, but my creative blocks have been removed. I have a spiritual vitality flowing all around and through me.

I believe I am a manifestation purposed by the Creator Designer. I am part of his field of energy with the invaluable privilege to self-reflect. Now, in all of creation, I see more reflections of this Designer Self. In every encounter, I seize the social opportunity to reflect on my nature and the Higher Nature. In recognizing myself in others, my identity expands. In doing so, I realize that up until this point, I have lived a life of artificial limitation.

I aspire to experience myself in all things until I find the fullness that will become my truer sense of self. Then, I will no longer see myself through my father's dreams, current profession, African heritage, Southern birth, male gender, or American nationality. Then, I'll be another in a line of available actors cast on the stage of the universe, currently playing a role, but no more identified with it than Angela Bassett identifies as Tina Turner. I now believe that my previous perception of myself as separate from the whole was my greatest ignorance.

AFFIRMATIONS

I am a part of the essence of the universe.

I am connected to the natural flow of life.

I am grateful for my soul's projection.

I choose to find beauty in every experience.

I am investing in my eternity.

I am an expression of perfect love to all creation.

MEET THE AUTHOR

Chauncey is the son of LaVerta Moore and Dave McGlathery, the former pastor of Pine Grove Missionary Baptist Church and a pioneer in the civil rights movement. His father launched Chauncey on a path towards the destruction of all barriers to wealth and wellness. He is a licensed and ordained minister in the Mallard Creek Primitive Baptist Association here in Huntsville. He trained at Auburn University School of Engineering, earning a Bachelor of Science Degree in Electrical Engineering, Howard University School of Law, earning a Doctor of Jurisprudence and Beeson Divinity School, earning a Masters of Divinity.

Chauncey was admitted to the federal bar of the Southern and Eastern Districts of New York and practiced law with some of the most well known civil rights attorneys in the country. He was a member of the Special Federal Litigation division and specialized in Section 1983 of Title 42, which allows federal review of alleged state civil rights violations. While in New York, Chauncey defended the City of New York and its Police and Correction Departments in civil rights cases under the Giuliani administration. While in Boston, Chauncey received additional leadership training from many institutions including Harvard University, Tufts University and the Interaction Institute. Most recently he served as an adjunct professor in the African and African Diaspora Studies Department at Boston College. He currently owns his own business consulting practice based here in Madison County, specializing in the fields of organizational development, executive benefits, Medicare and health and life insurance. He continues his work in the community by showing business leaders how to use the principles of faith in their everyday lives and business decisions. Chauncey is currently working on his second book, *Burst Your Own Bubble: Create a Mindset for Better Outcomes*.

STAY CONNECTED

Thank you for reading, *The Hero's Journey: Deliver Yourself from Evil.* Chauncey looks forward to connecting with you. Here are a few ways you can connect with the author and stay updated on new releases, speaking engagements, products, and more.

FACEBOOK	Chauncey ofThe MindfulFamily
INSTAGRAM	@chaunceymcglathery_
WEBSITE	www.chaunceymcglathery.com
EMAIL	cm@chaunceymcglathery.com